PRAISE FOR 30 WORDS

"Jarrid Wilson has a passion and heart for God that is contagious. His genuine faith comes through powerfully in his teaching and writing. *30 Words* points to the God of all wonder and grace in a way that will expand your faith and experience of God."

—Jud Wilhite, senior pastor of Central Christian Church, and bestselling author of *Pursued* and *Torn*.

"Jarrid Wilson has something beautiful and encouraging to say about the heart of God, and people are definitely listening. His passion, honesty, and insights are having a profound impact on our generation, and it is an honor to call him my friend."

—Mike Foster, author of *Freeway* and *Gracenomics*

"Jarrid Wilson is a passionate emerging voice on a relentless mission to point everyone to Jesus. *30 Words* will help you experience Jesus more deeply, as it did for me."

—Gene Appel, senior pastor of Eastside Christian Church, and author of *How to Change Your Church (Without Killing It)*

"*30 Words* is an amazing read—a must read. The simplicity makes it attractive and encouraging. Jarrid did a great job in providing the reader with confidence to live by faith."

—Aaron Curry, NFL linebacker

"Jarrid is such a solid, genuine man of God. He is a great inspiration and example to many people. *30 Words* Rocks! It will open your mind and allow you to dig deeper in your faith."

—Zac Archuleta, professional skateboarder

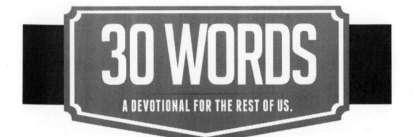

30 WORDS

A DEVOTIONAL FOR THE REST OF US.

JARRID WILSON

KIRKDALE PRESS

ACKNOWLEDGMENTS

To my parents. Thank you for your constant encouragement and
support. You are two of the greatest role models in the world.
I would not be where I am today without you.
Thank you for always being there.

*To my family, friends, blog readers, Twitter followers, and Facebook
friends.* Thank you for consistently supporting me throughout
my writing journey. This book would not have
been possible without your support.

CONTENTS

INTRODUCTION

Almost five years ago I told myself I would one day write a book. I didn't necessarily know when that day would come, but it gives me great joy to say you are currently reading that book. I didn't know what this book was going to be called, be about, or look like. But what I did know was this: It was going to be written to help people far from God find identity in Jesus Christ.

Don't get me wrong, I'm no Spurgeon, Kempis, Moody, or Chambers. But I will tell you this: God has given me a calling that I cannot ignore, and a purpose that I cannot turn away from. This book is just a beginning to the vast amount of things I wish to accomplish for the name of Jesus. But before I get carried away, I want you to understand that this book is not about me. This book is about you, your purpose, and your relationship with God.

By reading one "word" every day for 30 days, my hope is that you will be encouraged, inspired, and convicted to dive into a deeper relationship with God—and not just because me, your pastor, spouse, small-group leader, or parents are telling you to. But because *you* have personally decided to open up your heart to the immeasurable beauty of God's being.

Nothing in this world compares to what God can offer you. And no matter how familiar you are with the Bible, I pray this devotional will help bring you a fresh wind of encouragement and wisdom.

We all have goals, ideas, and the innovation to dream big, but where is the line between dreaming it and achieving it?

The idea of "having faith" is something we often throw around. Our culture has deemed "Just have faith" as the answer to just about every problem that does not have a clear solution. And although I do believe our faith is an unprecedented foundation in our walk with Jesus, faith without internal or external initiation is profitless. We can say, "I have faith," but if our hearts and souls aren't ready to prove otherwise, what good is it? Faith is a living, bold trust in God's grace, so certain of God's existence that it would risk death a million times.

Looking back to Scripture, a man named Peter gives us a wonderful example of faith initiation. Although Peter was mocked on various occasions for his innocence of stature, he was a faithful servant who loved Jesus with all of his heart. Matthew 14:25–29 paints a beautiful picture of Peter's faith and trust in Jesus. He is given the opportunity to internally and externally initiate his faith by stepping off the safety and comfort of his boat. Amidst the crashing of waves and rolling of thunder, Peter takes a step of faith toward the ultimate goal: Jesus.

We can make fun of Peter all we want, but if we're really honest with ourselves, I don't see anyone else faithful enough to step off that boat. Sometimes having faith means engaging in something so bold that you will end up looking stupid if Jesus doesn't come through.

The reality is, we all want to walk on water, but none of us wants to step off the boat. It's time to initiate our faith. It's time to step off the boat. Faith is the vision of the heart; it sees God in the darkest of times as well as in the brightness of days.

Ultimately, hearing the Word initiates faith; speaking the Word activates faith; doing the Word demonstrates faith.

VERSE OF THE DAY – JAMES 2:17

"So you see, faith by itself isn't enough. Unless it produces good deeds, it is dead and useless."

CHALLENGE

Tweet or post, "God doesn't lack in answer of prayers, we just lack in the art of true faith. #30WordsBook"

DISCUSS

1. Rate your faith on a scale of 1–10. Be honest.

2. What is something you've done recently to demonstrate your faith?

3. Discuss examples of bold people who have expressed their faith throughout Scripture.

REFLECT

Hearing the Word initiates faith;
Speaking the Word activates faith;
Doing the Word demonstrates faith.

Questions:

1. when all is well - 10
   when it might cost me - 4

2. prayed w/ a stranger in an
   elevator

3. Noah, Abraham, Moses,
   Joshua (battle of Jericho)
   Esther, Ruth

Jer. 29:11 For I know the plans I
have for you, declares the Lord, plans
to prosper you & not to harm
you, plans to give you hope
& a future.

When I truly trust Jer. 29:11 it is
easy to have faith.

Question: What do all of these have in common?

- Tofu
- Veggie burgers
- Mountain lightning
- Substitute teachers

Answer: They are all substitutes for the original. And regardless of their value as a substitute, most substitutes are portrayed as "Just the same," or "As good as the original." But in reality, are they? Not usually. (Except for maybe substitute teachers. Everyone loves them.)

Substitutes and replacements are everywhere. And although many of us don't realize it, much of our lives are spent trying to fill voids with substitutes and replacements rather than reaching for the real stuff.

The question I'd like to propose is this: Are we doing the same with God?

Although money, jobs, titles, and successes aren't necessarily bad things, when they start becoming our source of worth, they have become a worthless attempt in replacing the fulfillment of God—the only true fulfillment.

The reality is, you can't replace the irreplaceable. God is unending, all powerful, and life giving. To think that we could replace His love with something of this world immediately forfeits our belief in His power and majesty.

VERSE OF THE DAY - FIRST TIMOTHY 2:5

"For there is only one God and one Mediator who can reconcile God and humanity—the man Christ Jesus."

CHALLENGE

Tweet or post, "There is no replacement for He who is irreplaceable. #30WordsBook"

DISCUSS

1. What other things can you name that have substitutes?

2. What things in your life do you consider irreplaceable?

3. Can anything in this world offer what God can give us?

1.

2. my husband, children, memories, photos

3. of course not but it doesn't mean I won't try.

REFLECT

_____

_____

_____

_____

_____

_____

_____

_____

_____

_____

_____

_____

_____

_____

_____

_____

All of us were once children, unable to feed ourselves, clean ourselves, or even take ourselves to the bathroom. And while you might not remember much of your time as a child, I can guarantee you that somebody at some point took care of you. Whether through the provision of food, shelter, or care, we've all experienced a time in our lives when we relied on someone else because we could not provide for ourselves.

In Scripture, we find that Jesus is our ultimate provider. Not only because He provided redemption and mercy on the cross, but because everything given to us was never really ours in the first place. Everything good comes from Jesus, and we cannot say we truly love Him until we can humbly accept this beautiful reality.

Like any loving parent, our Heavenly Father is looking to provide for His children. In fact, in Hebrew, the term *Yahweh Yireh* means "God our provider." And although we all have different needs, God has the omnipotent power to take care of every single person who calls upon His glorious name. Nothing is too big or too small.

The voice of God has the power to raise the dead, yet sometimes we still worry if God will come through in our measly troubles. If Martha could meet Jesus on a hot dirty road and believe that He could raise Lazarus from the dead (John 11:17–27), what's stopping us while we sit in our comfortable houses from believing He can provide our most simple of needs? Look at all the things Jesus provided during His time on earth:

- Food for the masses (Luke 9:10–17)
- Calming of storms (Luke 8:22–25)
- Healing for the sick (Luke 14:1–6)
- Healing for the lame (Matthew 15:30)
- Protection for those amidst hardship (Isaiah 33:21)

You get the point. Many of today's Christians are focused on obtaining what they want instead of being content knowing God will provide for their needs. He is our ultimate provider, and without Him we are nothing more than children grabbing for things we cannot reach.

"And this same God who takes care of me will supply all your needs from his glorious riches, which have been given to us in Christ Jesus."

CHALLENGE

Take some time to thank God for His provision. Write down five things that He has provided you with, and three things you desperately need provision for. Pray over these three things for the remainder of the month and seek guidance in God's provision.

DISCUSS

1. How has God provided for you lately?

2. In what ways do you need provision in life?

3. Discuss instances where God has provided for His people in Scripture.

1. materially; grace; wisdom of my husband
2. daily needs; forgiveness
3. 40 yrs in the desert,

REFLECT

Provided me w/:

1. husband, children, parents, family, etc...

2. friends

3. a ~~hospitable~~ home; a hospitable spirit (or the gift of hospitality)

4. ability to stay home; raise our kids

5. a good marriage

Need provision for:

1. wisdom for fostering

2.

It just struck me that the "Ultimate Provider" (God) once needed to completely be provided for, needed to depend on someone

The phrase "Live like Jesus" is something we as believers always hear, but do we really understand what it means? Are we really living a life that radiates Christ? And are we truly abandoning our fleshly desires to pick up the cross that changed the destiny of all humanity?

When I was younger I once heard a pastor say, "Partial obedience is disobedience." And while everyone around me began to get up from their chairs, clapping and saying, "Amen!" I quietly sat in my seat. The phrase smacked me across the face and pierced me to the core. It is so true. I've realized we cannot go about our lives half-hearting our walk with God in hopes that He will give us a full-heart transformation.

If we are truly living like Jesus, then why are we still sinning? The depth behind the phrase "Live like Jesus" is immeasurable. And although this is a great starting point for our relationship with Him, truly understanding its meaning is more beneficial than aimlessly trying to accomplish its task. Yet so many of us are running around like a chicken with its head cut off, only hoping we are living like Him.

The reality is, God never intended for us to remain the same; He intended for us to remain obedient. For in remaining obedient, we will not remain the same.

Jesus wants us to find our divine purpose of living like Him. In doing so, our lives will have a lot more purpose and a lot less confusion.

"For merely listening to the law doesn't make us right with God. It is obeying the law that makes us right in his sight."

CHALLENGE

Tweet or post, "Partial obedience is disobedience. #30WordsBook"

DISCUSS

1. Rate your obedience to God's instruction on a scale of 1–10. *Be honest.*

2. In what ways can we show our obedience to God's instruction?

3. Discuss instances in Scripture where people have not followed God's instructions. How did their situations turn out?

3.ᴬ Moses - didn't get to go into the Promised Land

ᴮ Ananias & Saphira

REFLECT

_____

_____

_____

_____

_____

_____

_____

_____

_____

_____

_____

_____

_____

_____

_____

The change of the world started with Jesus, and ultimately it will end with Jesus. But the real question is, what lies in between those two paradigms?

All throughout Scripture we indefinitely see that we are called to be like Jesus; we are called to be the difference, and until Jesus returns in glorious fashion, we are called to *be the change*.

What does that mean?

It can be something as simple as letting your voice be heard, or even being a little louder than you were the day before. The point is, we are all on different spiritual levels, but we are all called to be the change, and that's one thing that won't ever change. The reality is, everyone is looking for change. But until someone does something about it, those things that need to be changed will never change. Make sense?

Our world relies on a sense of comfort, and in that, change is the last thing we want to think about. Although adding something different to your life can most of the time be good thing, research estimates that millions of people fear change. This fear is also known as "neophobia"—yes, it's a real phobia, and yes, it shows how faithless we really are.

My point: We are so comfortable in where we are that we ignore openings that might help us get where we are heading. We all want change, but we are scared to be the ones to step out and *be the change*. We can't expect to look any different than the world while we continue to bathe in the same junk as it.

We've created an agenda of comfort that keeps us from breaking into the world of "changedom" (yes, I invented that word). If we want change, we need to be the change we want to see. God hasn't called us to conform to the patterns of this world, but to be transformed through the sacrifice of Jesus Christ. This means:

Refuse to be average, and let your heart soar as high as God will allow it.

EVALUATE

We all make mistakes. We all screw up. We all fall short. But in the core of your heart, do you understand what it means to be a follower of Jesus? And based on your everyday lifestyle, do you reflect that identity?

- Are you living for God?
- Have you been transformed?
- Are you living different from the world?

VERSE OF THE DAY - ROMANS 12:2

"Don't copy the behavior and customs of this world, but let God transform you into a new person by changing the way you think. Then you will learn to know God's will for you, which is good and pleasing and perfect."

CHALLENGE

Tweet or post, "I will be the change. #30WordsBook"

DISCUSS

1. In what ways can we "be the change?"

2. Are today's Christians making a change in the world?

3. What are some concrete ways you can inspire change in your community?

REFLECT

"What oxygen is to the lungs, such is hope
to the meaning of life."

—Emil Brunner

Have you ever felt hopeless, worthless, or just downright useless? I believe we all have those days, months, or even years where we feel like we are nothing but a shadow in a world of color—like our existence means nothing, or that the day of our birth was a catastrophic mistake in the time continuum.

And while all those things might feel very real to you, I am here to tell you that they're wrong. In fact, they're straight up lies.

Check this out: Jeremiah 1:5 states, "I knew you before I formed you in your mother's womb. Before you were born I set you apart and appointed you as my prophet to the nations." Did you catch that? God knew you before He formed you in your mother's womb. He knew you before you were born. And on top of that, He set you apart from the beginning of time to be someone of substantial worth in His name.

Bam! Take that hopelessness!

God is the author of all hope. Hope brightens the darkened soul; it breaks the slave's chains; it sustains those in spiritual exile, comforts those in a place of suffering. When our hope is in God, our spirits cannot be crushed.

Here's my point: Today is a day to focus on the hope that God has purposed for your life. It is the day to break away from the lies of Satan and to realize you are purposed for a life with God. Don't let the opinions of people interfere with the directions given to you by God.

Does this mean things are going to be perfect? No, but this does mean that you have someone in your life who gives you worth, acceptance, and love.

"I say to myself, 'The LORD is my inheritance; therefore, I will hope in him!' "

CHALLENGE

Tell a stranger that your hope is found in God. Share the hope of your Savior to someone who has yet to know it.

DISCUSS

1. Share a time when you felt hopeless or helpless. What happened, and how did you handle the situation?

2. How can we as Christians strengthen our hope in God's presence, God's purpose, and God's eternal promise?

3. What is the content of Christian hope? What are we hoping for?

REFLECT

Ask yourself these questions:

- Are you truly a Christ follower?
- Can you honestly call yourself a Christian?
- Have you truly surrendered your life at His feet?

In our fast-paced world of technology, Starbucks, and tweets, I think we've lost sight in what God is truly yearning for. And although He loves us, cares for us, and showers us with His grace, God wants to be our entire life—not just a part of it.

In the eyes of God, there is no such thing as a partial surrender. It's all or nothing. Christ fully died on a cross, and it's our calling to fully live for him. He is not just an addition, He is the solution. And there is nothing more fulfilling than knowing your life and future are in the hands of Jesus.

Consider Jesus' words in Matthew 16:24–25: "Then Jesus said to his disciples, "If any of you wants to be my follower, you must turn from your selfish ways, take up your cross, and follow me. If you try to hang on to your life, you will lose it. But if you give up your life for my sake, you will save it." A life reflecting Jesus is one built upon a foundation of surrender. Let go and embrace the will of God.

"O my son, give me your heart. May your eyes take delight in following my ways."

CHALLENGE

Evaluate every aspect of your life, and ask yourself, "Is there more I could be surrendering to God (time, money, gifts)?"

DISCUSS

1. Discuss ways you've surrendered to God.

2. What does the phrase "surrendering to God" mean to you?

3. Have you truly surrendered your entire life at the feet of God?

REFLECT

Prayer is one of those things that from the outside might seem a little complicated, but in all reality, it is a simple way of communicating with our Heavenly Father. Just like any other conversation with someone you love, prayer is an intimate time of communication when we truly get to learn about one another. And although God already knows everything there is to know about us, prayer is given to us as a gift to learn about Him.

Martin Luther King, Jr. once said, "A Christian who does not pray is like a man who does not breathe; they cannot survive." Prayer is the life source between us and God. And although today's culture has turned prayer into nothing more than a nighttime ritual, I believe God is looking for a lot more than that.

In order for us to understand the basics of prayer, today I want us to unveil the reality of what prayer actually is. Are you ready?

Prayer is a conversation between you and God.

Simple, right? Yet so many of us ignore the opportunity to communicate with God because we feel like we have everything under control, or maybe because we feel like our issues are too small to be bugging the creator of the universe with. But in all reality, that's the beauty of God. He is big enough to handle the big, and He is loving enough to handle the small. Nothing is insignificant in God's eyes. He comes with open arms and an open heart, yearning for our affection and love.

It is intrinsic for God to want to help us. Why? Because any loving father would want to help his children, no matter the situation.

Don't get me wrong, prayer is not synonymous with "wishes" spoken to a magic genie. God is anything but a bald guy in a magic box. Prayer is your opportunity to wholeheartedly release your life into the hands of the one who created it. It's a time to open your soul to someone who knows it better than you ever could. And it's a gateway to gaining a deeper relationship with the one who knows our worth.

"I love the LORD because he hears my voice and my prayer for mercy."

CHALLENGE

Take some extra time out of your day to spend time in prayer with God. It doesn't matter where you are or what time you decide to do it. Just simply talk to God and allow Him to reside within the core of your heart. This is one conversation you don't want to miss.

DISCUSS

1. On a scale of 1–10, how great is your prayer life? *Be honest.*

2. Discuss a prayer that God has answered for you.
   Discuss a prayer that God hasn't answered for you.

3. What is your motivation for praying? Has your motivation changed over the years?

REFLECT

> "I would rather make mistakes in kindness and compassion
> than work miracles in unkindness and hardness."
>
> —Mother Teresa

Jesus rose from the dead and freed us from the bondage of our sins. And by doing so, He opened the door for anyone wanting to find a relationship with His Father in heaven. Jesus' message has never changed. And to anyone who has never felt the warmth of compassion, His voice is calling out, wherever you might be.

Jesus' great desire is that you would come to Him with all your faults, all your cares, and all your struggles. He doesn't seek to harshly judge you, but to gracefully and compassionately help you. He wishes to take hold of your pain and shower you with unfathomable love and grace.

He speaks with a voice of compassion and understanding. He will lift you from the lowest of lows and bring light to your darkened soul. He died for all our mistakes, and He brings healing to all of our wounds.

Open your heart to Him. Trust Him with your pain and sorrow. To the hurting He brings comfort, and to the lonely He brings purpose. Jesus personally took upon Himself the grief of all people. He took our sicknesses and burdens, and He carried our sorrows upon His back. He proved Himself a true brother of love and character. A tear brought a tear into His eye, and a burden brought a hurt to His heart. He felt for those who didn't even know Him, let alone trust Him. The soul of Jesus was one of generosity, for He gave up all He had for people who did not deserve His sacrifice.

"Since God chose you to be the holy people he loves, you must clothe yourselves with tenderhearted mercy, kindness, humility, gentleness, and patience."

CHALLENGE

Tweet or post, "I will show compassion as Jesus has shown it to me. #30WordsBook"

DISCUSS

1. When is the last time you cried over someone going through a tough time?

2. Describe an opportunity you've had to be compassionate toward someone in need.

3. Do you believe Christians today are compassionate enough?

REFLECT

All throughout Scripture, we see Jesus using broken people to spread hope to a broken world. He didn't use the popular, rich, or successful, but rather the poor, broken, and faithful.

It doesn't matter where you've been, what you've done, or who you used to be. God can use all people for the good of His will. Just look at our heroes from the Bible:

- Abraham was prone to lying out of fear (Genesis 12:11–13; 20:2).
- Moses had a speech problem that left him insecure (Exodus 4:10).
- Gideon was afraid and skeptical (Judges 6:11–27).
- Rahab was a prostitute (Joshua 2:1).
- Noah got drunk (Genesis 9:20–21).
- Jacob was a liar (Genesis 27:1–29).
- David was a murderer (2 Samuel 11:1–26).
- Jonah ran from God (Jonah 1:3).
- Peter denied Christ—three times (Matthew 26:69–75).
- Zacchaeus was hungry for money (Luke 19:1–10).
- The disciples couldn't stay awake while praying (Matthew 26:36–46).
- Paul was once a persecutor of Christians (Acts 8:1–3).

If you ever feel like you aren't good enough, remember that Jesus used broken people to spread hope to a broken people. Jesus didn't call the equipped; He equipped the called.

Romans 8:28 states, "And we know that God causes everything to work together for the good of those who love God and are called according to his purpose for them." It doesn't matter how you grew up. It doesn't matter what you did or didn't do. It doesn't matter if you've been told, "You're too young," or "You're just like your dad." What matters to the world doesn't matter to God. And it's time you weave this very truth into the fabric of your heart.

Stop listening to the foolish lies of this world, and start appreciating and accepting the *truth* of God's Word. He wrote it for a reason, not for foolish speculation.

I'm sure you've encountered flaws, failures, and mistakes in your life. But that doesn't mean you have to stay that way. In fact, if you consider yourself a follower of Jesus Christ, you are called to overcome those very things. This does not mean you will find perfection, but you will undoubtedly find progress on the path of righteousness.

Just because it's how you grew up doesn't mean it's how you should stay. With Christ comes renewal and a new way of living. If God is your director, you won't be disappointed with the story called your life.

VERSE OF THE DAY - EZEKIEL 36:26

"And I will give you a new heart, and I will put a new spirit in you. I will take out your stony, stubborn heart and give you a tender, responsive heart."

CHALLENGE

Tweet or post, "My purpose is found in the name of Jesus. #30WordsBook"

DISCUSS

1. What do you believe God's purpose is for your life?

2. Discuss what has been a driving force in your life.

3. According to Jesus, how do we find our life purpose? What is required of us?

REFLECT

Waiting, waiting, and more waiting …

Waiting is something all of us do in life. And while some people like to claim that waiting is a great learning experience, in reality it feels more like a mental and emotional torture chamber.

To be honest, I dislike waiting. I've never been good at it. I've always liked to get things done as soon as possible and at a time that was most convenient to my schedule. In my impatience, what I fail to realize is that the fourth fruit of the Spirit is patience (Galatians 5:22). Christians are not called to be impatient people. Technically, the more we allow the Spirit to be active in our lives, the more patient in turn we should become.

Over the years I've realized that life doesn't revolve around me. Time does not click in parallel to my heart. And what I think, what I'm impatient about, will never be more important than what God already knows.

Have you ever been in a waiting room? You know, that smelly, dim room that feels like the black hole of all rooms? Regardless of why you are there, it's usually for a good reason. I can't really think of any waiting room that wasn't the step before hearing something of substantial value.

My point is, don't expect anything of substantial value to come out of a speedy process. I'm not saying it can't happen, but realistically, it won't. In fact, Scripture even promotes this (James 5:7–11).

Life is a waiting room, and patience is the antidote. Don't be in a rush to move forward when God might want you right where you're standing.

VERSE OF THE DAY - PROVERBS 21:5

"Good planning and hard work lead to prosperity, but hasty shortcuts lead to poverty."

CHALLENGE

Any time you feel impatience creeping within your bones, recite Proverbs 21:5 and pray for God to gift you with the blessing of patience. Remember, through patience and diligence, the snail reached the ark.

DISCUSS

1. Does today's society and way of living encourage us to be patient?

2. Discuss activities that require an incredible amount of patience.

3. Why does Scripture teach us that patience is such a vital part of our faith?

REFLECT

All of humankind is possessed with a tormenting disease called sin. On a daily basis we indulge in certain behaviors that will ultimately be our own demise (e.g., drugs, sex, alcohol, pornography, swearing, pride, lust, or selfishness). As Isaiah 64:6 declares, "We are all infected and impure with sin. When we display our righteous deeds, they are nothing but filthy rags. Like autumn leaves, we wither and fall, and our sins sweep us away like the wind."

It is within our human nature to live and work for ourselves. But within the confines of Scripture, we can find the guiding power to relinquish ourselves of these burdening attributes and find freedom from the bondage of our sinful nature. Take 1 John 1:7–9 for example:

> But if we are living in the light, as God is in the light, then we have fellowship with each other, and the blood of Jesus, his Son, cleanses us from all sin. If we claim we have no sin, we are only fooling ourselves and not living in the truth. But if we confess our sins to him, he is faithful and just to forgive us our sins and to cleanse us from all wickedness.

The more focused we are in the world, the less likely we are to do things that are holy. But the more focused we are on the cross, the less likely we are to do things that are sinful. Hebrews 12:2 offers us one more point of guidance: "We do this by keeping our eyes on Jesus, the champion who initiates and perfects our faith. Because of the joy awaiting him, he endured the cross, disregarding its shame. Now he is seated in the place of honor beside God's throne."

"But thank God! He gives us victory over sin and death through our Lord Jesus Christ."

CHALLENGE

Write down three sins you currently struggle with, and be honest about them with someone close to you. With that person, pray for eternal freedom from your current sins, and come to God with heart-filled surrender.

DISCUSS

1. What does "freedom in Christ" mean to you?

2. In what ways has Jesus shown you freedom in your life?

3. Discuss habits or sins from which you currently need freedom.

REFLECT

> "When we are powerless to do a thing, it is a great joy that we
> can come and step inside the ability of Jesus."

—Corrie ten Boom

I know sometimes we can get caught up in the motions of life, but I want to encourage all of us to continue our pursuit of Christ. Something my pastor said really put this into perspective for me. He said, "It's sad how many of us stop the pursuit once we've obtained what we want." He was referring to personal relationships and marriage, but I've realized we sometimes do the same thing when it comes to our relationship with God.

People come to find Jesus, but they fail to continue the pursuit once they "have what they want." We act like once we've found Him, we don't need to seek Him anymore. We don't necessarily say that, but we sure do act it. Yet God has called us to continually seek His face (Psalms 105:4). And although "continually" seems like a bit much, it's what He's called us to. We should *thirst* after time with our Father. There is nothing more fulfilling.

Believe me, I know sometimes things get crazy and hectic, but in reality, *we give time to the things we care about.*

Failing to spend time with God cannot be excused by lack of time or ambition. And when we do use those excuses, I believe Satan is at the core of them. Why? Because Satan doesn't want us spending *any* time with God. He shutters at the thought of another child being added into God's family.

Jesus didn't die so we could only spend five or ten minutes with Him a day. If you want a deeper relationship with God, stop digging through Scripture with a spoon. Open up and dig deep.

VERSE OF THE DAY - MATTHEW 6:33

"Seek the Kingdom of God above all else, and live righteously, and he will give you everything you need."

CHALLENGE

Start giving God more of your time, energy, and focus.
Allow Him the time He deserves, not just the time you have left.

DISCUSS

1. Discuss what it means to pursue God.

2. Name people throughout Scripture who pursued the presence of God.

3. In what ways does pursuing God strengthen our relationship with Him?

REFLECT

_____

_____

_____

_____

_____

_____

_____

_____

_____

_____

_____

_____

_____

_____

_____

_____

"Joy is the infallible sign of the presence of God."

—Pierre Teilhard de Chardin

Have you ever looked at the face of someone who just scored a winning touchdown, won first place at a competition, or just won the grand prize on a game show? Well if you have, I want you to realize that not one of those things has anything do with joy.

Why?

Because joy isn't a product of something you have your hand in. Joy is not affected by what we can do in our own strength. And joy is not something this world can truly offer us in the first place.

Most of us in today's world have mistaken happiness for joy. But if we really unveil the truth behind what joy in Christ is, it is something eternal and unshakeable.

What would happen if the man who scored the winning touchdown didn't get both feet on the field before the catch? What would happen if you took away the first place medal? And what would happen if the game show contestant had lost instead of won? Would those people still be "joyful?" Nope, because true joy cannot be taken away or affected by circumstances that surround us.

Joy is eternal. Joy cannot be shaken. Joy cannot be earned.

Imagine a world built on joy, and not the satisfaction of temporal happiness. Imagine if people found joy in simply living and weren't desperately searching for happiness by trying to make a living.

VERSE OF THE DAY - PSALM 16:11

"You will show me the way of life, granting me the joy of your presence and the pleasures of living with you forever."

CHALLENGE

Today, walk with the joy of the Lord. Keep your head high, vision clear, and heart pure. The joy of the Lord cannot be quenched.

DISCUSS

1. Discuss the difference between happiness and joy.

2. What blessings does God promise us that promote joy in our lives?

3. Can true joy be found apart from Jesus?

REFLECT

> "Being a disciple means being wrapped up in a story that isn't
> your own. As a disciple of Jesus you have given up all your
> rights and have been swept up into the grace of Jesus.
> The standout element of disciples, is that they make disciples.
> We can't truly say we've been enraptured by the story of Jesus
> if it isn't leaking out of our bones every second we get."

—Jefferson Bethke

To be honest, it took me about two years into my faith journey to truly understand what it means to be a disciple of Jesus Christ. In my defense, my confusion was caused by horrible examples of people calling themselves disciples of Jesus.

I soon realized that a disciple is a follower and learner of Christ, and that my mission as a disciple was to share the truth of Jesus and restore hope into a broken world. My calling as a disciple wasn't something I grew up thirsting to be. I like to say it chose me. Regardless of the initiation, those who call themselves followers of Christ have now enrolled themselves into a life of full-time discipleship. Not only are you a follower of Christ, but you are called to be a living example, a leader, and to build up other disciples around you.

Many of you might be thinking, "I'm not qualified for that." Remember this: God isn't looking to call the qualified; instead, He qualifies the called. Every step you walk as a disciple is a step in which you gain divine wisdom and guidance. And every day you walk alongside the glorious presence of Jesus is another day you will grow deeper as His disciple.

We have this idea that before entering into duty as a disciple, we need to be washed clean. But the reality is, we cannot prepare for what God will do in our lives because we are only as capable as God makes us. We must step up to the front of the battlefield ready to learn, seek, and ask. And although we may find failure amidst our journey, failure is a lesson learned in the eyes of God.

A disciple of Jesus is one who is willing to risk everything for the sake of sharing the hope of a man who can bring life to anything and anyone.

"Therefore, go and make disciples of all nations, baptizing them in the name of the Father and the Son and the Holy Spirit."

CHALLENGE

Make today your day to stand tall as a disciple of Jesus Christ. Seek His wisdom, guidance, and daily transformation.

DISCUSS

1. What does it mean to be a disciple of Christ?

2. To what length would you go to share the gospel of Jesus?

3. Discuss people in Scripture who risked their lives for the sakeof Jesus.

REFLECT

"God will never, never, never let us down if we have faith and put our trust in Him. He will always look after us. So we must cleave to Jesus. Our whole life must simply be woven into Jesus."

—Mother Teresa

"Never be afraid to trust an unknown future to a known God."

—Corrie ten Boom

Each of us has goals, dreams and ideas of what we want our futures to look like. But what happens when those things don't happen when we wish them to? It's really easy to love God when things are going just the way we want. But what happens when things don't work out the way we want? Does our faith, love, and trust in God decrease? Or does it stand strong, trusting all things are in His timing?

Sometimes, God will contradict our expectations for our own benefit.

I think we sometimes forget that God is all powerful, all knowing, and all capable. He isn't just a God of sometimes, but a God of always. As humans, we naturally feel let down when things don't go the way we want. But when did God ever promise to fulfill our desires in our time? He didn't.

In *Mere Christianity*, C.S. Lewis describes trusting in God in this way:

> To trust Him means, of course, trying to do all that He says. There would be no sense in saying you trusted a person if you would not take his advice. Thus if you have really handed yourself over to Him, it must follow that you are trying to obey Him. But trying in a new way, a less worried way.

God's promises are fulfilled in His time, His way, and for His purpose. And until we can let go and allow God's timing to reign number one in our lives, our relationship with Him is nothing more than shallow and transactional. It's time to put your trust in the only one you can always count on.

It's time to let go and let God be God. Trust in Him.

VERSE OF THE DAY - PROVERBS 3:5-6

"Trust in the LORD with all your heart; do not depend on your own understanding. Seek his will in all you do, and he will show you which path to take."

CHALLENGE

Tweet or post, "I will put my trust in God. #30WordsBook"

DISCUSS

1. Is it possible to consider yourself a Christian without trusting God?

2. Discuss why trust is such an important aspect to any relationship.

3. In what ways are you showing God that you trust Him with your life?

REFLECT

_____

_____

_____

_____

_____

_____

_____

_____

_____

_____

_____

_____

_____

_____

"Fear is a liar and a paralyzer. While we all deal with its crippling effects, we can't be defeated by it. Jesus empowered us through His sacrifice on the cross to break the chains of fear. By remembering that your faith in Christ is the ultimate defense mechanism, you will be given strength in the most difficult and scariest of times!"

—Ryan Wood

In life, we all have certain things we are afraid of. Whether those things are spiritual, emotional, or physical, fear can creep in at any time and stir up our insecurities. I know we all have human emotions, but when it comes to reaching an encounter with God, why do we sometimes find fear on the path?

In Scripture we constantly read stories of God protecting and rescuing His children. And although we know God is our protector, refuge, and strength (Joshua 1:9), we seem to forget these foundational qualities when faced with spiritual opposition.

Satan will do everything he can to get in the way of our spiritual confidence, and that includes using our feelings to distract the boldness and power of God's truth. Satan will whisper words of insecurity, saying "You're not strong enough," "You're not worthy," "You don't deserve this," or "You can't do this."

Don't let him or your emotions get the best of your best relationship with God. And don't let fear take away your focus on the promise of His word. Instead of listening to Satan's words, remember the words of 2 Samuel 22:3: "My God is my rock, in whom I find protection. He is my shield, the power that saves me, and my place of safety. He is my refuge, my savior."

Fear isn't in God's nature. In fact, fear cannot produce the holiness God wants to share with us because it is incapable of doing so. God has better things in mind for you than to fear. He wants you to know the depth of His love so completely that fear will have no place in your life.

VERSE OF THE DAY - JOSHUA 1:9

"Be strong and courageous! Do not be afraid or discouraged.
For the Lord your God is with you wherever you go."

CHALLENGE

Tweet or post, "I will fear NOTHING because NOTHING
is greater than my God. #30WordsBook"

DISCUSS

1. Discuss and examine your biggest fears in life.

2. Have you ever been afraid to try something new because you
   were concerned about the possible consequences?

3. What are some Bible passages you could use to encourage
   someone who was afraid to pursue God's calling in their life?

REFLECT

Have you ever noticed that God uses ordinary people to do extraordinary things?

No, seriously, think about it. All throughout Scripture we see tax collectors, fishermen, and physicians turned into gospel-preaching, truth-sharing world changers. How is this possible? Because the lives of these people have been empowered by the orchestrated truth of Jesus.

No matter who you are, where you've been, or what you've done, the love of Jesus will drastically change your life. I'm not talking about a minor tweak of self-worth and temporary fulfillment, but of a *heart* changing, *life*-altering experience that you can't find anywhere else. In Ezekiel 36:26, God describes this change: "I will give you a new heart, and I will put a new spirit in you. I will take out your stony, stubborn heart and give you a tender, responsive heart."

The gospel of Jesus is *not* a text book, but a life-book. It is filled with the innate wisdom, guidance, and beauty of a man who died for our sins so that we may live again.

When we value something through the eyes of God, we're able to see the extraordinary in something the world would call ordinary. While our world tries to keep quiet a truth that speaks volumes, our God continues to use ordinary people to do extraordinary things.

VERSE OF THE DAY - JEREMIAH 29:11

"For I know the plans I have for you," says the LORD. "They are plans for good and not for disaster, to give you a future and a hope. In those days when you pray, I will listen."

CHALLENGE

Tweet or post, "I am a child of God. I am NOT ordinary. I am extraordinary, and I serve an extraordinary God. #30WordsBook"

DISCUSS

1. What is something that, when viewed through the eyes of God, can be seen as extraordinary?

2. Why do you think God uses ordinary people to do extraordinary things for His kingdom?

3. Who in Scripture could be deemed as ordinary, but because of Jesus' calling in their lives, did extraordinary things?

REFLECT

"Gathering your self-worth externally is kind of like trying
to fill up a lake with a Dixie cup. It's just never enough.
That's why it's so addictive."

—Pete Wilson in his book *Empty Promises*

Usually when someone wants to get to know a person they've just met, they ask these three questions:

- Who are you?
- What do you do?
- Where are you from?

And although there is nothing wrong with asking these things, I believe our identities as Christians are to be built on a lot more than what can be answered in three shallow questions.

If we were to truly evaluate our lives, we'd all be surprised as to where we seek most of our identity. I'm not saying we do it on purpose, but many of us might be astonished to realize we're seeking our worth in the world around us, and not in the Savior who wants to breathe life into our hearts.

At the end of the day, the world can never offer anything remotely close to the worth and purpose of Jesus Christ. And if you don't believe me, ask one of the many celebrities who has everything by worldly standards but still feels alone, depressed, and unvalued. See? I told you so.

You can't find worth in a world built on worthless values—it's simply impossible. What people say has no power against what God already knows. Our worth is found in God, and our identity is found in His love.

You are uniquely made, destined for greatness, and have been set apart from the beginning of time (Jeremiah 1:5). While the world around you tries to fit you into the box of conformity, remember that God's yearning is for us to break that mold and be the change (Romans 12:2).

Your true identity is found in He who created you, not the world that tries to manipulate you.

"But we are citizens of heaven, where the Lord Jesus Christ lives. And we are eagerly waiting for him to return as our Savior."

CHALLENGE

Tweet or post, "My identity is found in Christ. #30WordsBook"

DISCUSS

1. What does it mean to find your identity in Christ?

2. Have you ever sought identity in something other than Jesus?

3. Discuss in what ways people try to find their identity in things other than Christ every day.

REFLECT

Our world has this crazy notion that once we seek God, everything will be hassle free. Now don't get me wrong, having Jesus in our lives makes a world of a difference. But don't be surprised if you hit obstacles the second you start to truly seek after God's heart. Just because God planned it doesn't mean Satan won't try to disband it. There are two things I know about Satan:

- He does not want me to be in a relationship with God.
- He will do everything he can to distract me from the truth.

Looking back at my past, I realize how many times I let Satan get in the way of my relationship with God. The sad part is, I always allowed it to happen when things were beginning to look bright. I've come to realize that my foundation in Christ wasn't based off my own personal relationship, but a reliance on others to help me construct it. Satan pushed that against me and used things like insecurities and past mistakes to keep me blinded from the truth.

Satan will do everything he can to distract us from the truth, because the truth of God is Satan's weakness. The truth of God is found in His Word (the Bible). And if we aren't willing to build upon that truth, then we aren't willing to accept the love and hope He has to offer. Our lives should be so infected with the love of God that we constantly yearn to read more, pray more, and praise more.

The truth of God is that all things must pass except the things that are of Him. In other words, God is the truth, and anything that is not of God will not be left standing in the end. Truth is not defined by our own subjective standards; it is determined by the source of truth Himself.

Ultimately, Jesus is not a concept or an idea; He is an eternal and unchanging truth. We might be free to reject a number of traditions, customs, and beliefs. However, we cannot make facts go away by ignoring their irrefutable truth. Whether we choose to believe or not, the fact remains that Jesus is Lord over all, believers and unbelievers alike.

Satan will try and distract you the second God's truth starts to attract you. Stand strong. Be courageous. Have faith. He is our foundation.

VERSE OF THE DAY - PSALM 31:4-5

"Pull me from the trap my enemies set for me, for I find protection in you alone. I entrust my spirit into your hand. Rescue me, LORD, for you are a faithful God."

CHALLENGE

Tweet or post, "God is truth, and truth is living. #30WordsBook"

DISCUSS

1. What does the truth of God mean to you?

2. Discuss in what ways the truth of God has changed your life.

3. In what ways has Satan tried to dismember the truth of God in our culture?

REFLECT

It's the thing that keeps you up at night and wakes you up in the morning. It's that thing that is always running through your mind, and somehow always finds its way into conversations. It's that constant tug that always has your mind running at 100 mph. And it's that thing that you will always stand up for, no matter the consequences. That is your passion.

Whether it be a social initiative, a job, or caring for the needy, we all have something that we feel is worth living for and ultimately worth dying for. What are you passionate about?

Passion can sometimes be confused with lustful desire, and I want this entry to help distinguish the two.

Passion without sacrifice is not passion; it is plagiarism of the heart. Passion is so much deeper than a transactional act. It is a selfless art of living, seeking the best for something or someone while disregarding any self-return.

In reference to our relationship with God, it may seem that obedience to God is the result of our passion for Him, but in reality, the opposite is actually true. If you come to Christ from an emotional perspective, your passion for God will be a result of your obedience and time spent with Him.

The reality is, Jesus brutally died on a cross, sacrificing Himself, because His passion was to bring us hope. He wasn't seeking transactional return or favor, but that we would find comfort in His forgiveness and eternal hope.

What could we possibly have to offer He who created the world? Nothing. Our number one passion should be directed toward the man who was nailed to the cross. True passion isn't trendy; it's never-ending, and it's never fleeing.

"Think about the things of heaven, not the things of earth."

CHALLENGE

Write down three to five things you are passionate about and pray over the ones you believe God has truly called you to pursue. True passion cannot be shaken.

DISCUSS

1. What passions has God has instilled in your heart?

2. How can we decipher between God-given passions and lustful desires?

3. Is passion enough? What other steps are needed to fulfill our callings in life?

REFLECT

Regardless of your religious beliefs, attempting to kill your only son because someone told you to will always sound a little bit strange. It's because of this that the story of Abraham and Isaac is one of the most controversial and discussed stories of all biblical text.

I'm not trying to bash this story. I believe it paints a powerful picture for us in regard to our faith, making us consider to what extremes we would go to prove our faith.

Here's the back story: God has continually promised Abraham an heir through his wife, Sarah; He has also promised Abraham that his descendants would come through this son. When she is 90 years old, Sarah gives birth to Isaac. Then, not long after this, God calls Abraham to offer up his only son as a worthy sacrifice. Genesis 22:9–10 describes the experience:

> When they arrived at the place where God had told him to go, Abraham built an altar and arranged the wood on it. Then he tied his son, Isaac, and laid him on the altar on top of the wood. And Abraham picked up the knife to kill his son as a sacrifice.

The word "sacrifice" can be defined as giving up something for the sake of something or someone else. God requests that Abraham sacrifice the very thing he loves dearly to test whether Abraham fully trusts in Him and has placed his heart fully in Him. He is looking for Abraham to prove his faith.

From Abraham's story, we see just how epic of a statement a sacrifice can make. We also get a picture of just how much God loves us: He spared Abraham from having to give up his son, but for us, God sacrificed His only son so that we could know Him.

How much would you sacrifice for someone you loved? What would you give up to prove your love for God?

VERSE OF THE DAY - ROMANS 12:1

"And so, dear brothers and sisters, I plead with you to give your bodies to God because of all he has done for you. Let them be a living and holy sacrifice—the kind he will find acceptable. This is truly the way to worship him."

CHALLENGE

Give up something you know is hindering your relationship with God. It may be something as simple as TV, or something as harmful as drugs. Regardless, anything hindering your relationship with God is something you can live without. Today is your day to make a change for the better and step into a new way of living.

DISCUSS

1. Discuss things you have sacrificed in your own life to show your dedication to God.

2. What are some things you believe you still currently need to lay down at the foot of the cross?

3. Can true love exist without some sort of sacrifice? Why would Jesus sacrifice Himself on a cross to show His love?

REFLECT

God spoke into motion the universe that astronomers estimate contains more than 100 billion galaxies. The combined energy of all the earth's storms, winds, ocean waves, and other natural forces cannot even come close to the almighty power of God.

While reading Scripture, we see that the Bible promises, "Now all glory to God, who is able, through his mighty power at work within us, to accomplish infinitely more than we might ask or think" (Ephesians 3:20). Although we as humans think we are great in our own power, in reality we are nothing compared to the almighty strength of the one who placed us into being.

Our all-consuming God is capable of doing anything He pleases. And in reality, He never fails, and He is never tired. No matter what you might be facing, God can help you. Philippians 4:13 reminds us, "For I can do everything through Christ, who gives me strength." Nothing is too hard for Him. No need is too great for Him. No enemy is too strong for Him to defeat. No problem is too complicated for Him to solve. And no prayer is too difficult for Him to answer.

Job 12:14–15 describes God's awesome power: "What he destroys cannot be rebuilt. When he puts someone in prison, there is no escape. If he holds back the rain, the earth becomes a desert. If he releases the waters, they flood the earth." Our God is the mightiest of all spiritual, physical, and emotional forms. And until we can truly accept this fact, a dividing line will hinder us from truly experiencing the beauty of God's presence.

VERSE OF THE DAY - PSALM 147:4-5

"He counts the stars and calls them all by name. How great
is our Lord! His power is absolute! His understanding is
beyond comprehension."

CHALLENGE

Today, focus on God's power. Don't try to do things on your
own. Initiate God's power in your life by putting your faith in the
power of His promise.

DISCUSS

1. Discuss and evaluate examples of God's power
   throughout Scripture.

2. How is God's power different or the same as the power
   of people today?

3. How can we begin to see our own weaknesses as God's power?
   Where have you seen this in your life?

REFLECT

"Without worship, we go about miserable."

—A. W. Tozer

Worship is something that might seem a bit confusing, but in reality, it isn't. It is within our human nature to worship something or someone. But the sad fact is, there are more than 600 different religious denominational churches, each with different doctrines and beliefs, who are attempting to worship God in ways contrary to what He says in the Bible.

The act of worship is to show respect, honor, or homage to a certain object or person. An in regards to our faith as Christians, our worship is to be directed toward our Lord and Savior. Worship is a time when we pay deep, sincere, awesome respect, love, and fear to the one who created us.

Our worship not only honors and magnifies God, but it is also for our own edification and strength. Worship helps us develop a God-like and Christ-like characteristics. When we worship God we develop traits such as forgiveness, tenderness, justice, righteousness, purity, kindness, and love. All of these attributes are preparing us for eternal life in heaven with the Father, Son, and Holy Spirit.

Ultimately, the art of worship is something that we cannot truly understand until we take part in it. And although the act of worship might seem conservative and dry, there are many ways to worship our God in heaven. Worship itself is not just an act, but a lifestyle in which we can live.

As followers of Jesus Christ, we are to be living sacrifices (a form of worship) to the one above. Worship should cause us to reflect on the majesty and graciousness of God and Christ, contrasted to our own unworthiness.

VERSE OF THE DAY - PSALM 96:9

"Worship the LORD in all his holy splendor. Let all the earth tremble before him."

CHALLENGE

Honestly answer the following questions:

- Do you worship selflessly?
- Do you worship honorably?
- Do you worship respectfully?

DISCUSS

1. What does worship mean to you?

2. When somebody says the word "worship," what images typically come to mind?

3. How can we worship God throughout our everyday life, and not just while at church?

REFLECT

First Corinthians 13:4–7 tells us:

> Love is patient and kind. Love is not jealous or boastful or proud or rude. It does not demand its own way. It is not irritable, and it keeps no record of being wronged. It does not rejoice about injustice but rejoices whenever the truth wins out. Love never gives up, never loses faith, is always hopeful, and endures through every circumstance.

Love is one of those things that might seem a little cliché, but in all reality it's a foundation that God has called us to construct our lives upon. Not only are we called to love our Lord Jesus Christ, but we are also to love our neighbor as ourselves.

I know what some of you are thinking: "But you haven't met my neighbors, they're crazy!" or "But sometimes I just have a bad day. What then?" Although loving others might be hard to do sometimes, we need to remember that Jesus' statement to love wasn't a request; it was a command.

Ask yourself how you can you be a visual image of God's love today. When God desired to show us His love, He sent Jesus to die on the cross for our sins (John 3:16). This act was an incredible image of service, selflessness, and sacrifice—all done to show a tangible and visible image of the invisible God.

Be honest with yourself in answering these questions:

- Are you loving the way Jesus loved?
- Are you loving your neighbor as yourself?
- Are you reflecting an image of love in your everyday actions?

I truly believe that love without sacrifice isn't really love in the first place; it's kindness. The greatest example of true sacrificial love can be found within the blood of Jesus Christ. Be an example of love, and make sure you show those around you know how much you really care.

"We love each other because he loved us first."

CHALLENGE

Strive to be a visible, tangible, and reflective image of God. Allow God's presence to fill your heart and show itself through your actions. Be a living example of the living God. Today, do nothing but acts of selflessness.

DISCUSS

1. What does it mean to love your neighbor as yourself?

2. On a scale of 1–10, how well do you resemble the love of Jesus?

3. What does today's culture say about love? Does it resemble the love described in the Bible?

REFLECT

In today's fast-paced, entrepreneurial society, everybody has the urge to do things on their own. And although it may seem very noble to take on the world alone, is that really the way God has called us to live?

I mean, I get it. You want to prove to the world that you can do it on your own, that you don't need others, that you are capable of greatness alone. But if your goal is to simply prove you can do something on your own, is that noble or just prideful?

After reading and studying through Scripture, I really began to understand the importance of teamwork and community entrepreneurship. Just look at these examples:

- David conquered Goliath with the power of the Holy Spirit, not by his own strength (1 Samuel 17:37, 45–47).
- Noah built the ark with God's guidance (Genesis 6:11–17).
- Moses led the Israelites out of Egypt with God as his guide and the help of a sidekick named Joshua.
- Jesus preached the good news with the help of 12 disciples.

I think you get the point. Drop the pride. Let God guide you. Doing things on our own is exactly what the evil one wants us to do. Remember: We're all in this together. We have a mission. We are the Church.

VERSE OF THE DAY - PROVERBS 3:5-6

"Trust in the LORD with all your heart; do not depend on your own understanding. Seek his will in all you do, and he will show you which path to take."

CHALLENGE

Tweet or post, "I will stop trying to do things on my own. Even Jesus had 12 disciples. #30WordsBook"

DISCUSS

1. In what ways has God supported you throughout your life?

2. Why is encouragement and support so important to our lives?

3. Discuss instances throughout the Bible where God has given support to people in need.

REFLECT

> "The grace of God is infinite and eternal. As it had no
> beginning, so it can have no end, and being an attribute
> of God, it is as boundless as infinitude."

—Unknown

> "Grace is like the wind...It fills the sails of the weary, lifts the
> spirit of the broken and if you open the doors and windows,
> it will gladly come in."

—Mike Foster

Grace is a gift from God that can never be earned, no matter how great we think we are. It's a gift we do not deserve that was given to us amidst our failures, mistakes, and sins. And although we will continue to fall short to the glory of God, His never-ending grace surrounds us like the roaring ocean surrounds a piece of driftwood.

Grace is a love that has nothing to do with us but everything to do with the one from whom it derived: God. It is a powerful, divine, and vital piece of our existence, and it is the only reason we are able to open our eyes each morning. God's grace is more than a second chance; it's a third, fourth, and fifth. It's a love that keeps on giving, regardless of our past.

Today, take some time to focus on the word "grace," and allow God to reveal Himself to you in a whole new way. Every day you wake up is a gift, and what you do with that gift will show your true understanding of grace. God's grace is what provides you the opportunity to fulfill your purpose, and those two realities cannot exist apart from each other.

VERSE OF THE DAY - EPHESIANS 2:8

"God saved you by his grace when you believed. And you can't take credit for this; it is a gift from God."

CHALLENGE

Show someone grace who does not deserve it. Why? Because you didn't deserve it when it was given to you.

DISCUSS

1. What does grace mean to you?

2. Discuss an instance where someone has shown you grace when you didn't deserve it.

3. Are you taking advantage of the grace you have been given, or are you using it for the glorification of God?

REFLECT

_____

_____

_____

_____

_____

_____

_____

_____

_____

_____

_____

_____

_____

_____

_____

_____

_____

Consider these three questions:

- Do you call yourself a Christian?
- Do you believe in the power of God's word?
- Do you believe the Bible is the inerrant and inspired word of God?

If you answered "yes" to these questions, congratulations! You've just applied yourself to a lifetime of full-time ministry.

Some of you are thinking things like, "But I don't work at a church," or "But I don't work for a Christian company," or "But I don't have time." Let's study what it means to live a life for Christ.

Philippians 1:21 offers this definition: "For to me, living means living for Christ, and dying is even better." If you claim to be a Christian, your life is meant to be lived for Him. Meaning, you have all the time in the world to do what you've been called to do in the first place.

Galatians 2:20 states, "My old self has been crucified with Christ. It is no longer I who live, but Christ lives in me. So I live in this earthly body by trusting in the Son of God, who loved me and gave himself for me." If you claim to be a Christian, then it is no longer you who lives, but Christ who lives in you. It's His agenda, not ours.

Finally, Romans 8:28 reminds us, "And we know that God causes everything to work together for the good of those who love God and are called according to his purpose for them." If you are in Christ, God can use your current situation and workplace for *His* purpose, with no exceptions.

The reality is, we are all called to full-time ministry, no matter where we work. Jesus isn't hiring part-time followers. Make it count.

"O LORD, I am your servant; yes, I am your servant, born into your household; you have freed me from my chains."

CHALLENGE

Don't let anyone tell you that full-time ministry can only be found within the confines of a church building. God is bigger than four walls and a steeple. Take your current situation and workplace as your personal mission field. Why? Because you can reach people a church can't. You're on the front lines! And make it personal. God has put the people around you in your life for a reason. Find out what that reason is, and make it your mission to empower people's lives with Christ.

DISCUSS

1. Discuss ways we can serve others in the likeness of God.

2. How does serving others provide meaning and purpose to you?

3. How does serving others provide meaning to the people you serve?

REFLECT

Did you know?

- 163,000 Christians die every year for their faith.
- 75 percent of all religious persecution in the world is against Christians.
- In the 20th century, more Christians died for their faith than in all the other centuries combined.

What does your relationship with Christ really mean to you? To what degree do you care for Him? And how far would you really go to share His love? Our natural instinct as Christians is to express that we love Jesus with our hearts and that nothing will stop us from proclaiming His name. But when it really comes down to it, is that true?

Paul, an apostle of Jesus, was a man who was beaten, stoned, and imprisoned for more than five years because of his proclamation of love toward Jesus. Nothing could break his love for Christ because a true foundation of Christ cannot be broken.

Is your life so infected with the love of Jesus that you would be willing to take beatings, mockery, and even torture? Are we truly sold out for the one who paid the price? And are we as Christ followers ready to die for the very person who died for us?

These are not hypothetical questions. They are real—just like the Love of Christ.

EVALUATE

- How much is your relationship with God worth to you?
- Are you willing to risk everything for the sake of Jesus?

VERSE OF THE DAY - MATTHEW 5:10

"God blesses those who are persecuted for doing right, for the Kingdom of Heaven is theirs."

CHALLENGE

Take time out of your day to pray for those who are being persecuted in the name of Jesus, and evaluate how much your relationship with Christ really means to you.

DISCUSS

1. Why is taking risks important to our relationship with God?

2. What lessons have you learned about taking risks and stepping into God's plan for your life?

3. Discuss people throughout Scripture who took risks in the name of Jesus.

REFLECT

> "The will of God will never take you to where the grace of
> God will not protect you. To gain that which is worth having,
> it may be necessary to lose everything else."

—Bernadette Devlin

Have you ever been so scared that you couldn't move, talk, or even breathe? Have you ever been in a situation where you didn't think you would make it out alive? Or have you ever been in a scenario where your worst fears in life actually became a reality?

All of us have imaginary situations we pray will never come true. But what if I told you that you didn't have to fear anymore? What if I told you that you have someone on your side who overpowers any opposition that comes in your sight? And what if I told you that the same person who is here to protect you is actually the same person we didn't protect on the cross? Ironic, huh?

Psalm 91: 1–6 provides us with a description of God's protection:

> Those who live in the shelter of the Most High will find rest in the shadow of the Almighty. This I declare about the LORD: He alone is my refuge, my place of safety; he is my God, and I trust him. For he will rescue you from every trap and protect you from deadly disease. He will cover you with his feathers. He will shelter you with his wings. His faithful promises are your armor and protection. Do not be afraid of the terrors of the night, nor the arrow that flies in the day. Do not dread the disease that stalks in darkness, nor the disaster that strikes at midday.

God is our lifeboat in a raging ocean, our shield against a powerful army, and our light amidst the uncertain darkness. God is our safe haven in our times of trouble. And in reality, the closer we are to the Shepherd, the safer we are from the wolf.

We are called to be dependent on God alone. For only God is faithful in all things, present at all times, powerful in all places, and mediator between earthly and heavenly realms. Do not fear the past, present, or future. Instead, throw yourself upon the mercy of our faithful God and know, deep in the core of your soul, that whatever happens—expected or shocking, next to you or on top of you, today or tomorrow—that you are safe in the arms of God.

VERSE OF THE DAY - PROVERBS 18:10

"The name of the LORD is a strong fortress; the godly run to him and are safe."

CHALLENGE

Tweet or post, "My safety is found in the arms of my father in heaven. #30WordsBook"

DISCUSS

1. What does being in the safety of God mean to you?

2. Discuss an instance where you truly felt the safety and comfort of God's presence.

3. In what ways does God provide safety for people throughout Scripture?

REFLECT

FINAL REFLECTIONS

_____

_____

_____

_____

_____

_____

_____

_____

_____

_____

_____

_____

_____

_____

_____

_____

_____

_____

AUTHOR'S NOTE

Now that you've made it through *30 Words*, I hope you're inspired to continue on your spiritual journey. There is no end to a relationship with God, and no limit to how much you can learn from the Bible. That's why we still study it thousands of years after it was written!

So, what's the next step?

The reason I decided to sign with Kirkdale Press is that it's a part of Logos Bible Software, a company dedicated to helping people learn more about the Bible and grow in the Word. If you're interested in learning more about the Bible, I strongly encourage you to visit Logos.com to find the Scripture software that's right for you. And if you want to read more teachings and studies on the Bible, I've compiled a list of books I recommend at JarridWilson.com/reading-list.

Most importantly, just keep pursuing Jesus.

Thank you, from the bottom of my heart.

—Jarrid

THANK YOU

Kaylie Wilson

Christian Wilson

Luke Wilson

Ryan Wilson

Jake Wilson

John Cassetto

Mike Foster

Jim Gray

Jefferson Bethke

Mike Worley

Aldo Daniel

Jud Wilhite

Ketric Newell

Jake Smith Jr.

Ross Kenyon

Celina Kenyon

Matt Morgan

Joel Piper

John Cassetto

Mike Foster

Jim Gray

Jefferson Bethke

Mike Worley

Gene Appel

Nita Grantham

Aldo Daniel

Jud Wilhite

Ketric Newell

Jake Smith Jr.

Adam Carpenter

Tom Wilson

Cyndi Wilson

Jason Kayser

Shane Lemmon

Austin Lemmon

Ronny Roa

Chuck Booher

Pam Booher

Jamie Martinez

Jami Passmore

Lori Klingsborn

Eric Klingsborn

Elizabeth Lunsoford

Katie Louise

Tony Wood

Casey R Marion

Jacob Everett Wallace

Kaylynn Gomez

Kevin Chatham

Jessica Alhanouch

Neah Elizabeth Sheets

Jared Mills

Glori Roldan Vargas

Du-Ann Renolda Daniel

Amber Smith

Jazmin Salazar

Ashlee Halocene Doherty

Laura Anderson

Brooke A. Scott

Yianna A. Segarra Torres

Kassey Tingler

Nikki Roethler

Alexandra Morales

Chantal Legere

Mikael Solis

Sabrina Marciella Delisfort

Loretta Rodriguez

Elsie Queenlouise Aimable

Omaira Daniela Velazquez

Shereyah Barnhart

Becky Jones

Carlos Erazo

Brice Wilson

Wendy Wilson

Carien Smith

Ashlyn Cara Troutman

Brittany Dawn Richards

Misty Rose Smith

Joshua Caines

Joy Defrane

David Defrane

Oliver James Jackson

Jessica Dai

Dennise Medeiros

Kristyn DeAnn York

Tj Cabacungan

Antonio Lattimore

Matthew Benavides

James Rensink

Julia Rensink

Jill Torley

Sonia Heredia

Logan Smolchuck

Magui Quintana

Garid Beeler

Kayla Gratoppi

Daniel Martinez

Angelica M. Guzman

Pamela Hamman

Sofia Araceli Mendoza

Cody Lee Simmons

Robert Keaton Washburn

Erica Chavez

Scott Corgan

Jim Del Campo

Vanessa Rodriguez

Jean Thompson

Rebekah Anne Holmes

Daniel Willian Ellison

Austin Nicholas

Ian Diorrio

Candys Chavez

Kastle Aarin Jones

Naomi Paul

Wyatt Lane Platte

Alicia Cheyenne Dueul

Georgia Rae Roppolo

Lauren Nichole Beck
Yvonne Zecua
Caitlin Emfinger
Lauren Harrell
Sarah Klarner
Bethany Calman
Rebecca Ashmore
Christine Reyes
Dani Catherine
Darren Wymer
Nathalie Roa
Kayla Dunn
Andrea Marbach
Edgar Sincel
Brittane Turner
Michelle Dubois Cuevas
Anthony Ibarra
Taylor Townsend
Krystle Raghoonanan
Elizabeth Ma
Natalie Bullis
Rennee Jakobi
Karla Leones
Leah Spellings Young
Kelsey Stark
Belinda Milan
Sharmela Rivera
Michelle Nagel
Tyler Inman
Ruby Vargas
Jefrey Cubero
Rosie Farias
Brandon Crespo
Ruthy Rodriguez
Trina Renee
Esmeralda Zecua
Selina Starr Cintrol
Astrid Calderon
Junior Vang
Kristiana Perkeci
Carly Guerro
Gabe Leyva
Taylor Reil
Kevin Rufus Bedford
Karine Goulet

Christian Spivey
Lisa Wood
Allison Dark
Brooke Ventimiglia
Mitch Demko
April Hill
Hailey Heckman
Crystal Ward
Ruth Ondevilla
Elizabeth Reth
Kevin Uffelman
Hannah McLarnin
Kayla Nicole Sparks
Cameron Lim
Brian Leake
Ronnie Bingaman
Shirley Snover
Berenice Santos
Orfalinda Serrano
Katherina Henson
Adriana Sanchez
Emili Hilde
Jacob Osborne
Holli Mediana
Mickey Estep
Abigail MacDougall
Travis Hurley
Natalia Hornsby
Yioma Rodz
Marinelle Tenorio
Alyssa Ponce
Gabriel Chang
Cristie Freeman
Timmothy Smith
Ester Gomes
Jane Baldwin
Maleny Davila
Ileana Reyna
Sarah Swain
Gina Ware
Jessica Andrews
Yossenia Lotta
Lauren Elizabeth Menke
Julie VanGyzen
Stephanie Robinson

Kristina Murahov
Amanda Teeter
Tamara Swoager
Allura Garia
Ashley David
Ashley Flow
Logan Kelley
Samantha Rench
Yeager George
Elioenai Ibarra
Kayla Wilkins
Crystal Geraldson
Tory Howard
Zack Tuen
Aaryck Enriquez
Mj Wilkins
Timothy Lee
Jarid Stone
Love Kovalchuk
Logan Moses
Anne Bracero
Thea Gomez
Gretchen Tenorio
Tessa LaCorte
Renata Machado
Rebeca Flores
Shiela Marie Rota
Oneta Okwufulueze
Mary Sanchez
Ruth Vazquez
Brizza Martinez
Tania Salas
Jay Wright
April Gardner
Ryan Drake
Joy Lantu
Mark Willians
Ace Pampolina
Kathy Curley
Sari Gunawan
Briannah Dickson
John Tumilty Spykman
Skylar Rains
Nicole Brokenshire
Catherine Garcia

Ashley Cox
Ada Fernandez
Gina Jackson
Jared Eckert
Amanda Cordova
Nokuthula Mtembo
Diana Alvarez
Andrew Columbia
Herlin Puspasari
Michelle Herr
Lu Allan
Diana Gualteros
Tayo Ajala
Kayla Stimmell
Kristin Sagebarth
Juliany Gonzalez
Emily Masich
Kidron Stamper
Joanne Marie Krayer

Sarh Rupp
Paola Grillo
Janjan Rajel
Vicka Marko
Sharlie Peterson
Andriana Ochoa
Mokaro Osazuwa
Christy Evangelin
Claudine Cook
Jesca Viduya
Kristin Leigh Mapili
Kimolan Perumaul
Ria Tan
Nadine Pillay
Danelle Frans
Angelica Terraza
Joy Sacbibit
Ina Marrica Shayla
Maha William

Zoe Louella Quirk
Olivia Tung
Shannon Caffey
Jeremy Rivera
Jamie Quinn
Anabel Carrasco
Meghan Ray
Michele Martinez
Jeremy Carpenter
Macy Groves
Joshua Jones
Kiersten Boyer
Timmy Timbit
Amy Graybill
Lou Capeda
Nanci Priscila Lopez
David Martin
Hannah Crews

ABOUT THE AUTHOR

Jarrid Wilson is a pastor, blogger and author whose motivation is to help others find their identity in Christ. In 2010 Jarrid helped assist a church plant in Orange County, CA and is now continuing his pursuit in sharing the hope of Jesus to the world. Jarrid is currently studying biblical studies and theology through Liberty University, and he plans to continue his education by obtaining a Master of Divinity. Using creative, outside-the-box perspectives, Jarrid is passionate about connecting God's Word to the upcoming generation through relevant, yet challenging and pivotal messages. Speaking life and hope through social media networks such as Twitter, Facebook, and his blog (JarridWilson.com), Jarrid is determined to use every avenue available to audaciously shout the truth of a loving and personal God.